Jewish Life in Ancient Egypt is made possible, in part, by The Joseph S. and Diane H. Steinberg Charitable Trust, The Judy and Michael Steinhardt Foundation, The Leo and Julia Forchheimer Foundation, Jeannette and Jonathan Rosen, and Meridian Capital Group. Additional support is provided by the Barbara and Richard Debs Exhibition Fund of the Brooklyn Museum of Art.

Support for this publication was provided by a BMA publications endowment created by the Iris and B. Gerald Cantor Foundation and The Andrew W. Mellon Foundation.

Jewish Life in Ancient Egypt is made possible, in part, by The Joseph S. and Diane H. Steinberg Charitable Trust, The Judy and Michael Steinhardt Foundation, The Leo and Julia Forchheimer Foundation, Jeannette and Jonathan Rosen, and Meridian Capital Group. Additional support is provided by the Barbara and Richard Debs Exhibition Fund of the Brooklyn Museum of Art.

Support for this publication was provided by a BMA publications endowment created by the Iris and B. Gerald Cantor Foundation and The Andrew W. Mellon Foundation.

Jewish Life
in Ancient Egypt

Jewish Life in Ancient Egypt

A Family Archive from the Nile Valley

Edward Bleiberg

BROOKLYN MUSEUM OF ART

Published on the occasion of the exhibition *Jewish Life in Ancient Egypt: A Family Archive from the Nile Valley*, organized by the Brooklyn Museum of Art and on view from February 15 to May 12, 2002.

The exhibition is made possible, in part, by The Joseph S. and Diane H. Steinberg Charitable Trust, The Judy and Michael Steinhardt Foundation, The Leo and Julia Forchheimer Foundation, and Meridian Capital Group. Additional support is provided by the Barbara and Richard Debs Exhibition Fund of the Brooklyn Museum of Art.

Support for this publication was provided by a BMA publications endowment created by the Iris and B. Gerald Cantor Foundation and The Andrew W. Mellon Foundation.

This publication was organized and printed at the Brooklyn Museum of Art
James Leggio, Head of Publications and Editorial Services and project editor
Project art director: Harold Wortsman
Designer: Christine Staehelin

ISBN 0-87273-147-2

The translations printed in this volume are adapted from Emil G. Kraeling, *The Brooklyn Museum Aramaic Papyri: New Documents of the Fifth Century B.C. from the Jewish Colony at Elephantine* (New Haven: Published for The Brooklyn Museum by Yale University Press, 1953).

All objects illustrated are in the collection of the Brooklyn Museum of Art.

Photograph Credits: Dean Brown, pages 11–13, 20, 22, 31. German Archaeological Institute, Cairo, page 15. Betty Leigh Hutcheson, pages 2, 10, 14, 17–19, 25, 27, 29, 33, 35, 37, 40, 43.

Frontispiece: *Persian Guard*. From the Audience Hall (Apadana) at Persepolis. Reign of Xerxes (486–464 B.C.E.). Limestone, 10½ × 9 × 2 inches (26.6 × 22.8 × 4.7 cm). 65.195, Gift of the Kevorkian Foundation in memory of Hagop Kevorkian

CONTENTS

FOREWORD

The group of Aramaic papyri belonging to the Brooklyn Museum of Art, around which we have organized the exhibition *Jewish Life in Ancient Egypt*, provide unique, tangible, and astonishing confirmation of the Biblical narrative, in II Kings and Jeremiah, that Jews were again living in Egypt during the fifth century B.C.E. Though archaeologists are unable to confirm the Biblical account of the first sojourn of Jews in Egypt and the Exodus, these papyrus documents demonstrate that Jews returned to Egypt centuries later, after the destruction of Solomon's Temple in Jerusalem in 586 B.C.E., and became well-integrated into Egyptian society.

The Brooklyn papyri are famous among scholars, but until now the public has heard little about them. Yet these extraordinary documents have a fascinating story to tell. They comprise the archive of one Jewish family living in Egypt between 449 and 402 B.C.E. and record such turning points in their domestic lives as arranging a marriage and purchasing a house. The family included Ananiah, a Jewish priest; his Egyptian wife, Tamut; and the children they raised in a town on Elephantine Island, near Egypt's border with Nubia. In the exhibition, selected works of art from the Museum's Department of Egyptian, Classical, and Ancient Middle Eastern Art give a broad cultural context to the family documents. Together, the documents and related objects illuminate a little-known but important period in both Egyptian and Jewish history. They tell an unexpectedly detailed, true-life story more than 2,500 years old.

I am particularly grateful to Edward Bleiberg, a member of our distinguished team of curators of Egyptian art, whose leadership and focused intellectual energy brought this important project to fruition, to the benefit of all who will learn from it. Indeed, *Jewish Life in Ancient Egypt* demonstrates, once again, the richness of the Brooklyn Museum's collections and the rewarding opportunities they hold for the public we serve. I am indebted as well to Rabbi Shalom Levine and the Library of Agudas Chassidei Chabad, Ohel Yosef Yitzchak–Lubavitch for graciously lending three rare, historic Haggadoth that enlarge the scope of the exhibition.

The Museum's superb staff has once again created an exhibition and catalogue that are both engaging and informative. Special thanks for turning the idea behind the exhibition and book into a reality go to Simon Adlam, Michael Blakeslee, Joel Hoffman, James Leggio, Caroline Lu, Kenneth Moser, Stefania Rosenstein, Eileen Willis, and Harold Wortsman. The administrative development of the project was skillfully supported by Judith Frankfurt, Cynthia Mayeda, Marc Mayer, and Kevin Stayton. Many other members of our staff participated in essential ways in producing this exhibition; they include Walter Andersons, Dean Brown, Lisa Bruno, Reggie Cameron, Sara Caspi, Kevin Cooper, Kristi Dahm, Rachel Danzing, John DiClemente, Peter Downes, Keith DuQuette, David Geiger, James Gordon, Adam Husted, Hiroko Kariya, David Kleiser, Elaine Komorowski, Robert Krulak, Marilyn Kushner, Sarah Kutner, Phyllis Kwalwasser, Deirdre Lawrence, Gary Logan, Giuseppe Luciani, Tina March, Hannah Mason, Melissa Mates, Barbara Head Millstein, Travis Molkenbur, Sara Moy, Won Ng, Antoinette Owen, Judith Paska, Ellen Pearlstein, Kate Portada, Katrina Posner, Dominick Prisco, Liz Reynolds, Cynthia Silva, Gregg Stanger, Peter Trippi, Eddy Trochez, Robin Weglinski, Sally Williams, and Kathy Zurek. Beyond the Museum's staff, thanks are also extended to Christine Staehelin, who designed this catalogue; Betty Leigh Hutcheson, who provided additional photographs reproduced here; and Noah David Smith, who made the exhibition's video.

I am enormously grateful for the trust that enlightened philanthropists place in us. Their trust strengthens our resolve to create innovative, thoughtful exhibitions and programs of the highest intellectual and artistic quality. Very special thanks are due The Joseph S. and Diane H. Steinberg Charitable Trust, The Judy and Michael Steinhardt Foundation, The Leo and Julia Forchheimer Foundation, and Meridian Capital Group for the generosity that made the exhibition possible. Additional support was provided by the Barbara and Richard Debs Exhibition Fund of the Brooklyn Museum of Art. Funding for this catalogue was provided by a BMA publications endowment created by the Iris and B. Gerald Cantor Foundation and The Andrew W. Mellon Foundation.

For the ongoing support of the Museum's Trustees, we extend special gratitude to Robert S. Rubin, Chairman, and every member of our Board. Without the confidence and active engagement of our Trustees, it would not be possible to initiate and maintain the high level of exhibition and publication programming exemplified by *Jewish Life in Ancient Egypt*.

Arnold Lehman
Director, Brooklyn Museum of Art

Map of ancient Egypt with an inset showing Elephantine Island, where the Brooklyn Museum papyri were discovered

INTRODUCTION

And the entire people, from the smallest to the biggest, and the officers of the soldiers, arose and came to Egypt, because they were afraid of the Babylonians.
(II Kings 25:26)

By the rivers of Babylon / There we sat / Also we wept / When we remembered Zion.
(Psalm 137)

Twelve hundred years after Joseph, his father, Jacob, and his brothers first entered Egypt, and eight hundred years after Moses led the Exodus, Jews were settled in Egypt again. Following the period of turmoil that witnessed the destruction of Solomon's Temple in Jerusalem, some Jews came back to Egypt once more, lived active lives, and practiced their own form of worship.

Through the nearly miraculous preservation of hundreds of papyrus rolls from one Jewish settlement on Elephantine Island in the Nile River, scholars have been able to reconstruct the texture of Jewish life in ancient Egypt during this latter period, in the fifth century B.C.E. Many of these documents, known as the Elephantine Papyri (pronounced Elephan-*tee*-nee), are now in museums in Berlin and Oxford. An important group of eight of the papyri, discovered in 1893, entered the Brooklyn Museum of Art's collection in 1947, along with a number of related fragments.

The eight Brooklyn papyri concern one particular Jewish family, providing specific information about the daily lives of a man called Ananiah, a Jewish temple official; his wife, Tamut, an Egyptian slave; and their children, over the course of forty-seven years. This family archive is the central focus of *Jewish Life in Ancient Egypt*. In addition, selected objects recovered through archaeology as well as a close reading of the Hebrew Bible and Egyptian inscriptions further reveal the world the family lived in. Their society included Jews, Egyptians, and Persians living side by side in relative peace. All three groups led productive lives and worshipped their gods, free from religious persecution.

Jews Return to Egypt

The history of Jewish resettlement in the Nile Valley began late in Egypt's Dynasty 26 (664–525 B.C.E.). By that time, only the Kingdom of Judah remained of the larger state that the Biblical kings Saul, David, and Solomon had ruled successively three hundred years earlier. The political situation in Judah was grave. King Necho of Egypt (Figure 1) killed King Josiah of Judah during a battle at Megiddo (610 B.C.E.), part of a long war caused by shifting alliances among Egypt, Assyria, and Babylonia, the great powers of the day. Josiah's death set in motion a series of events that led to the Babylonian conquest of Jerusalem (586 B.C.E.) and the destruction of Solomon's Temple. At that time, the Jewish population was dispersed to Babylonia and Egypt: the intellectual and economic elite of Judah was exiled to Babylonia, while the soldiers and common people escaped to Egypt. The Jews in exile in Babylonia went on to develop the intellectual basis of their faith and ultimately provided the principal source of modern Judaism; the Jewish remnant in Egypt continued to practice the older polytheism and ritual of the Judean and Israelite countryside.

Figure 1. *Statuette of King Necho.* Provenance not known. Late Period, Dynasty 26, possibly reign of Necho II, circa 610–595 B.C.E. Bronze, 5½ × 2¼ × 3 inches (14 × 5.7 × 7 cm). 71.11, Charles Edwin Wilbour Fund

Figure 2. *Soldiers Honoring Their Lord.* From Saqqara; probably from the tomb of Horemheb. New Kingdom, late Dynasty 18, reign of Akhenaten (circa 1352–1336 B.C.E.) or Tutankhamun (circa 1336–1327 B.C.E.). Limestone, painted, 16½ × 14½ inches (41.8 × 36.6 cm). 32.103, Charles Edwin Wilbour Fund

The Persians, a new power on the scene, in turn conquered Babylonia in 539 B.C.E., and Egypt, too, became part of their empire in 525 B.C.E. The Persians permitted the Jews of Babylon to return to Jerusalem and rebuild the Temple, where these Babylonian Jews established normative beliefs and practices. Other Jews, however, remained in Egypt. In Elephantine Island, these Jews were members of the mercenary forces guarding Egypt's southern frontier (Figure 2). They lived among the native Egyptians, the Persians who had now conquered Egypt, and Greek mercenaries in a multicultural and multilingual society. The amicable way of life of these peoples reveals the wisdom of the Persian policy of religious tolerance, benefiting both Egyptians and Jews.

Egypt During Persian Rule

The [Persian] King Cambyses came to Egypt. . . . He gained mastery over this entire land. . . . I made his royal title as King of Upper and Lower Egypt Mesuti-re ["Offspring of Re"]. (Inscription of Udjahorresnet, an Egyptian official)

The Egyptian elite regarded their new Persian rulers, Cambyses among them, as traditional pharaohs. Some officials who had served Dynasty 26 kings continued in office during the First Persian Period (Dynasty 27). They adopted a Near Eastern style of dress (see Figure 3) that was already known in Egypt in Dynasty 26, and they wore typically Persian jewelry. Though mid-twentieth-century commentators anachronistically labeled these officials "collaborators," the concept of nationalism did not exist before the invention of the modern state. Rather, ancient elites were primarily concerned with economic security. As for the common people, it made little difference to them whether those who collected the taxes were ethnic Egyptians or Persians.

After the period featured in *Jewish Life in Ancient Egypt*, there was a brief return to native Egyptian rule in Dynasties 28 to 30 (404–343 B.C.E.), followed by the short-lived Second Persian Period (Dynasty 31, 343–332 B.C.E.). Then life in Egypt changed drastically once again, when Alexander the Great (Figure 4) conquered the country in 332 B.C.E. His successors were the Macedonian Greek pharaohs who built the new city of Alexandria; Egyptian Jewish history would enter yet another new phase when large numbers of Jews from Egypt and from the east settled there.

Figure 3. *Ptahhotep, Overseer of the Treasury, in Persian Costume.* Probably from Memphis. Late Period, early Dynasty 27, First Persian Period (circa 525–404 B.C.E.). Graywacke, 32½ × 10½ × 12⅝ inches (83 × 27 × 32.1 cm). 37.353, Charles Edwin Wilbour Fund

Figure 4. *Alexander the Great.* Provenance not known. First century B.C.E.–first century C.E. Egyptian alabaster, 4 inches (10.5 cm) high. 54.162, Charles Edwin Wilbour Fund

The Story of Ananiah and Tamut

And Johanan son of Kareah and all the chiefs of the military forces and all the people did not obey the voice of Jehovah to keep dwelling in the land of Judah. . . . And they finally came into the land of Egypt. (Jeremiah 43:4, 7)

And Jehovah will send you back to Egypt . . . in the road that I had told you that you would never see again; and you will have to sell yourselves there to your enemies as slaves, and there will be no buyer. (Deuteronomy 28:68)

The Hebrew Bible gives dire warnings, such as these, about the Jews' return to Egypt. Yet the hundreds of papyri discovered on Elephantine Island in Egypt tell a different story. The papyri reveal a prosperous community integrated into its surroundings. And they allow scholars to reconstruct specific lives within the larger historical context of invasions and conquests.

13

Figure 5. *An Ancient Family: Stela of User-pekhty-nesu and Netjer-pay, His Wife.* From Saqqara. New Kingdom, Dynasty 18, circa 1539–1513 B.C.E. Limestone, 14½ × 10 × 3 inches (36.8 × 24.8 × 7.5 cm). 37.1353E, Charles Edwin Wilbour Fund

We know that most of the Jews in Elephantine were soldiers. However, Ananiah, the original owner of the eight papyrus scrolls housed in the Brooklyn Museum of Art, was not a soldier. He was a temple official, active between 449 and 402 B.C.E. The papyri allow us to retrace the events of his life during that period of forty-seven years in some detail: he marries a woman named Tamut; the couple then buy a house, raise a son and daughter, and try to help the growing children establish themselves in their own lives. It is a story that could be a modern movie. The characters in the story include:

Ananiah, a Jewish official at the Temple of Yahou (Jehovah)

Tamut, an Egyptian slave and wife of Ananiah

Palti, their son

Yehoishema, their daughter

Ananiah son of Haggai, their son-in-law

Meshullam, Tamut's master

Zakkur, Meshullam's son

Tamut's natural father had sold her into slavery, probably to pay his debts, sometime before the story begins. From then on her master, Meshullam, functioned legally as her father, while Meshullam's son Zakkur had the legal responsibilities of a brother to her. To understand this situation, we need to remember that slavery in ancient Egypt differed from the kinds of slavery in history with which we may be more familiar: Egyptian slaves could own property, have professions, and be entitled to compensation. A slave like Tamut could, moreover, marry a free person, but her children still belonged to her master, their legal father.

We do not know how Ananiah and Tamut met. Their village was small, though, and they probably had known each other since childhood.

Figure 6. Modern excavation of the town of Khnum on Elephantine Island, Egypt

Ananiah must have spoken Egyptian and Aramaic, two of the languages used in Elephantine. As was typical in the ancient world, the relationship between Ananiah and Tamut had been established for quite some time before they formed a legally recognized marriage. The couple's son, Palti, was about six years old when Ananiah and Meshullam, as Tamut's legal father, wrote the marriage contract. (In Elephantine, an Egyptian marriage agreement differed from a Jewish one: an Egyptian agreement was made between the man and the woman [such as the couple in Figure 5], while a Jewish agreement was between the man and his father-in-law.)

The story told by the papyri properly begins when Ananiah formally marries Tamut in 449 B.C.E. Their marriage contract includes a clause freeing their son, Palti, from slavery. The contract, however, does not free Tamut herself: Meshullam remains Tamut's owner and legal father. Perhaps it is the desire to free the six-year-old Palti that leads Ananiah to accept the small bride-gift of 15 shekels from Meshullam (or possibly as little as 7 shekels; the text is ambiguous).

15

Twelve years later, in 437 B.C.E., Ananiah purchases a dilapidated house in the town named for the god Khnum on Elephantine Island (Figure 6). He then spends some of his time repairing it, and after three more years, in 434 B.C.E., gives title to part of the house to Tamut. He is perhaps thereby celebrating the birth of their daughter, Yehoishema; giving such a gift upon the birth of a child is a common custom in the community. The document conveying title to Tamut mentions Yehoishema as the natural daughter of Ananiah, but legally still the daughter of Meshullam.

A few years further on, in 427 B.C.E., the family has reason to celebrate again, as Meshullam frees both Tamut and Yehoishema from slavery. The documents do not indicate the reason for this event.

We know from a fragmentary papyrus not included in the exhibition that there is another celebration in July 420 B.C.E.: at that time, probably anticipating her marriage, Ananiah gives Yehoishema title to part of the house. In October of the same year, Yehoishema formally marries a man who is also named Ananiah (he is distinguished here from her father by the added phrase "son of Haggai"). Her marriage contract with Ananiah son of Haggai specifies that her own property is worth 78.125 shekels. This marriage property comes to Yehoishema from Zakkur, still her legal brother through her former enslavement. The amount of the property suggests that the family has come far since the mother's marriage, when Tamut had brought only 7 or 15 shekels with her. Yehoishema will be given two more sections of the house by her parents in the course of her married life.

Yehoishema's document of title transfer records that her natural brother, Palti, had already received a portion of the house before Yehoishema's marriage. But Palti's document is not preserved in the archive. Perhaps documents pertaining to Palti's adult life would have been found in his wife's home; scholars have suggested that in marriages between two free individuals, in general the wife owned the house.

Sixteen years later, in November 404 B.C.E., Ananiah gives the now married Yehoishema an additional part of the house, and in March 402 B.C.E. gives her yet another part of the house. Then, in December 402 B.C.E., Ananiah and Tamut sell the final share of the house to their son-in-law, Ananiah son of Haggai. The family disappears from the historical record after that last preserved document. If Yehoishema and Ananiah son of Haggai had children, they are not mentioned in the archive. Archaeological evidence suggests that the Jewish community in Elephantine continued for several more generations; other Jewish communities in Egypt prospered into modern times.

•

Over the decades documented by the papyri, the way that the family's real estate dealings, in particular, are handled illustrates a remarkable degree of freedom: they owned property in a village where their immediate neighbors were both Egyptians and Persians. The documents demonstrate as well that both Jews and Persians could serve as witnesses to legal transactions. And it is notable that Tamut and Yehoishema's eventual freeing from slavery, like the other interactions with their non-Jewish neighbors, also reveals this lack of self-consciousness about ethnicity in legal matters. But perhaps the most "modern" feature of Ananiah and Tamut's world was its separation of religion from other aspects of life.

Religion in Elephantine

And now, this is what Jehovah, Lord of Hosts, the God of Israel, has said: "Why are you causing a great calamity to your souls . . . by making sacrificial smoke to other gods in the Land of Egypt?" (Jeremiah 44:7–8)

His Majesty [Darius] did this . . . in order to cause that the names of all the gods, their temples, their offerings, and the conduct of their festivals might endure forever.
(From the Inscription of Udjahorresnet, an Egyptian official)

Persian kings officially encouraged the worship of local gods throughout the empire. The chief deities of conquered peoples came to be associated with Ahura Mazda, the great god of the Persian pantheon. In broadest outline, religions in this period taught that animal, meal, and incense offerings to a god ensured protection in return. Their deities were both male and female and sometimes conceived of as family units, as was common in Egypt.

Figure 7. *Ram-Headed Egyptian God Seated on a Throne.* Provenance not known. Late Period, Dynasty 26 (664–525 B.C.E.) or later. Bronze, $3 \times 1\frac{1}{2} \times 1$ inches (7.8 × 4 × 2.3 cm). 37.682E, Charles Edwin Wilbour Fund

Figure 8. *Egyptian Priest Kneeling with Offering Table.* Possibly from Memphis. New Kingdom (1539–1075 B.C.E.) or later. Bronze, 2½ × 1 × 1⅜ inches (6.4 × 2.1 × 3.7 cm). 37.362E, Charles Edwin Wilbour Fund

In Elephantine, the Egyptians maintained the cult of the god Khnum, symbolized by the ram (Figure 7). Khnum's family included Anukis and Satis, two locally important goddesses. Khnum was worshipped nationally as a creator god but in Elephantine was especially revered as being responsible for the annual Nile flood that fertilized the land. Numerous ram mummies from the area attest to the practice of offering this sacred animal to the god. Other national deities, such as the goddess Mut, were also known at Elephantine, and sometimes honored through use in personal names.

Persian deities in Egypt at this time are also known from the papyrus documents. However, artistic evidence of Persian gods is rare, and difficult to interpret. The Persian king most likely practiced Zoroastrianism.

The local Jewish community worshipped "Yahou who is in Elephantine." This deity was, for them, synonymous with Jehovah (Hebrew: *YHWH*), the all-powerful creator of life. Yet in some respects they were virtually polytheists, as their near-contemporary, the prophet Jeremiah, charged in the passage quoted on the previous page, and they also worshipped Melqat-Ha-Shemayim ("Queen of the Heavens"), probably as Yahou's spouse; this goddess had a separate temple in Syene (Aswan), on the eastern bank of the Nile. The papyrus documents further attest that oaths were sworn in the names of a variety of other gods, such as Bethel. At his temple in Elephantine, Yahou was worshipped with animal sacrifices, as was the practice in the Temple in Jerusalem. For the most part, the worship of Yahou with animal sacrifice or the Queen of the Heavens with meal offerings would not have seemed unusual to the Jewish community's neighbors.

Ananiah was a member of the Jewish priesthood in Elephantine (Figure 8). He was "the *lechen* of Yahou the God who is in Elephantine." His wife, Tamut, bore the corresponding feminine title, "the *lechenah* of Yahou." The meaning of *lechen* and *lechenah* and other priestly titles in Elephantine is obscure. Priests in Assyria and Babylonia used the same title. In one instance, the *lechen* was responsible for temple maintenance and the care of the god's ritual utensils, garments, and jewelry (Figure 9). Other priestly titles used in Elephantine include *kohen*, for one who performed a traditional role in preparing the sacrifice, and *kemer*, a title also found in the Bible, but there associated with pagan gods.

Figure 9. *Bowl with Persian Decoration.* Said to be from Tell el Maskhuttah, Egypt. Late Period, Dynasty 27, First Persian Period (525–404 B.C.E.). Silver, 3 inches (8 cm) high × 7 inches (18.3 cm) diameter. 54.50.35, Charles Edwin Wilbour Fund

In death, at least some members of the Jewish community were buried in anthropoid stone coffins resembling those used by the Egyptians. Some went so far as to decorate the coffin with images of Isis and Nephthys, the Egyptian goddesses of mourning. Terracotta coffins are also known from this period (Figure 10).

Who Was a Jew in the Ancient World?

This description of Ananiah's practice of Judaism raises the question of who was a Jew in the ancient world. Modern Jews might not easily accept Ananiah, Tamut, and their children as being, in fact, Jewish.

Originally, the term "Jew" referred to people from the territory of Judah, part of the state ruled by the kings Saul, David, Solomon, and their successors. Today, it is a religious and ethnic designation; indeed, the ethnic use of the term "Jew" probably began during the First Persian Period in Egypt (Dynasty 27, 525–404 B.C.E.). Although the religion and rituals of the Jews of ancient Egypt might not seem completely Jewish to us, they shared much with Jews living today. They worshipped Jehovah—though with animal sacrifice, as did all Jews in Biblical times—and they observed the Sabbath and the Feast of Matzah (modern Passover). At the same time, they were products of a world much different from ours.

Figure 10. *Lid of a Sarcophagus.* Said to be from a Jewish cemetery at Tura, Egypt. Late Period (664–332 B.C.E.). Terracotta, 36 × 23 × 1 inches (92 × 58.5 × 3 cm). 37.1517E, Charles Edwin Wilbour Fund

The first difference lies in sacred scripture. The Jews of Elephantine certainly did not yet have the Talmud and other rabbinical interpretations of the laws of the Hebrew Bible. The rabbis wrote those texts hundreds of years after Ananiah and Tamut lived. Thus their practices should not be viewed through the lens of Rabbinical Judaism. It is also not clear whether individuals such as Ananiah and Tamut had the Torah (Law), Prophets, and Writings in the form that we know today as the Hebrew Bible. The canonical text of these books was not set until 70 C.E., more than five hundred years after Ananiah and Tamut lived. None of the Jews in Elephantine took names from the Biblical patriarchs Abraham, Isaac, and Jacob, suggesting that perhaps they were unfamiliar with the Book of Genesis as well. Instead of these, they usually took names compounded with Jehovah: Ananiah's name, for example, meant "Jehovah will answer" in Aramaic, while Yehoishema's name meant "Jehovah will hear."

Ananiah and Tamut's religious practice, too, would be unfamiliar to modern Jews. They worshipped at the "Temple of Yahou [Jehovah] who is in Elephantine." This was indeed a temple, where animal, grain, and incense sacrifices were made; not a synagogue, a place for study and prayer. None of the traditional life-cycle events of Rabbinical Judaism—B'rit milah (circumcision), Bar/Bat Mitzvah, marriage, or funerals—can be associated with the temple. It functioned, much like the Temple of Jerusalem, as a place for sacrifice.

The mixture of similarities and differences in scripture and rites suggests a complex, ambiguous state of affairs. When the prophet Jeremiah specifically condemned the practices of the Jews of Egypt, they could respond that theirs was an older form of worship, which Jehovah had always accepted. Clearly, even in the ancient world there were disagreements among Jews over religious practice.

•

It remains to be noted that Elephantine in the fifth century B.C.E. was one of the last communities to thrive before political anti-Semitism arose in the Hellenistic period and marred the lives of both Jews and gentiles. The religious tolerance that had been fostered and practiced by ancient Near Eastern peoples remains an ideal for the modern world.

Figure 11. *Statue of Amenhotep Son of Nebiry as a Scribe.* From Thebes. New Kingdom, Dynasty 18, Reign of Amunhotep II (1426–1400 B.C.E.). Limestone, 26 × 12½ × 14¾ inches (66 × 32.1 × 37.6 cm). 37.29E, Charles Edwin Wilbour Fund

THE FAMILY ARCHIVE OF ANANIAH AND TAMUT

Discovery of the Papyri

ASSOUN, January 26–February 13, 1893: All these papyri from Kôm, *shown me by three separate women at different times.*

(From the notebooks of Charles Edwin Wilbour [1833–1896])

Egyptian farmers discovered the archive of Ananiah and Tamut on Elephantine Island in 1893, while digging for fertilizer in the remains of ancient mud-brick houses. They found at least eight papyrus rolls, which were soon purchased by the pioneering American Egyptologist Charles Edwin Wilbour. Wilbour thought these papyri were written in "Phoenician," since he did not recognize the Aramaic script and similar papyri had not yet been found in Egypt. He did not show them to anyone outside of his family and put them in a tin biscuit box for storage. The biscuit tin was placed in the bottom of a trunk with his other Egyptian papyri. There it stayed, forgotten, after Wilbour's death three years later.

In 1947, Theodora Wilbour, Charles's daughter, donated the contents of the trunk to the Brooklyn Museum of Art. The papyri remained astoundingly well-preserved, with seven of the eight rolls still sealed. They were opened, studied, and published in 1953.

As described in the Introduction, these are the papyri forming the family archive of Ananiah, an official at the Temple of Yahou (Jehovah) in Elephantine, and his Egyptian wife, Tamut. Unfortunately, the Brooklyn papyri, so famous to scholars, have until now remained virtually unknown to the public. Each of the eight papyri is reproduced and translated in the pages that follow. The papyri—which are, essentially, legal documents—have been grouped here by topic, such as marriage contract, real estate transaction, or loan agreement.

The Aramaic Language

[King Nebuchadnezzar] said to them: "There is a dream that I have dreamed and my spirit is agitated to know the dream." At that the Chaldeans spoke to the king in the Aramaic language.

(Daniel 2:3–4)

My father was an Aramean who was perishing, and he went down to Egypt to settle there . . .

(Deuteronomy 26:5)

The Brooklyn papyri were written in Aramaic, the daily language of the Jews and Persians of Egypt. The Biblical writers knew that the Chaldeans spoke this language and also thought the patriarchs spoke Aramaic. Outside the Bible, it is attested as the international language used by Assyrians and Babylonians beginning in the twelfth century B.C.E. Diplomats used Aramaic in the Persian Empire as late as the fourth century B.C.E. Dialects of Aramaic are still spoken today in Iraq and Syria.

Not only the Jews living in Elephantine in this period spoke Aramaic. It was also the language commonly spoken by the Jews of Jerusalem by 300 B.C.E. The Torah was translated from Hebrew into Aramaic for their benefit. Passages in the Biblical books of Daniel and Ezra were composed in Aramaic rather than Hebrew.

The Aramaic script in these papyri resembles the script used to write Hebrew.

Scribes and Literacy

Professional Aramaic scribes wrote out these documents. They used the same materials and reed pens as did Egyptian scribes (see Figures 11 and 12). The scribes were familiar with the legal formulas employed in real estate transfers, marriage documents, and loan agreements. A close look at the bottom of the papyri shows that the witnesses signed the documents in their own hands. These signatures suggest a rudimentary level of literacy among the Aramaic-speaking population; perhaps more people could read than could write.

24

Figure 12. *Scribe's Palette and Reed Pens.* From Elephantine Island, Egypt. Late Period, Dynasty 28–30 (404–343 B.C.E.). Wood, reeds, and ink, 5 × 1½ × ⅝ inches (12.6 × 3.5 × 1.75 cm). 16.99A–D, Gift of the Estate of Charles Edwin Wilbour

MARRIAGE DOCUMENT

Marriage Document of Ananiah and Tamut

Ancient marriage documents generally formalized already existing relationships. In this case, Ananiah and Tamut already had a young son when the document was drawn up.

Because Tamut was a slave when she married Ananiah, the contract has special conditions: normally, it was the groom and his father-in-law who made Jewish marriage agreements, but Ananiah made this contract with Tamut's master, Meshullam, who was legally her father. In addition, special provision was made to free the couple's son, also a slave to Meshullam; perhaps Ananiah consented to the small dowry of either 7 or 15 shekels (the text is ambiguous) in order to obtain his son's freedom. Future children, however, would still be born slaves.

In contrast to Jewish documents like this one, contemporaneous Egyptian marriage documents were negotiated between a husband and wife.

Translation:

[Date:] *On the 18th [of Tammuz {Aramaic calendar}, that is the 3rd day] of the month of Pharmouthi [Egyptian calendar], the 16th year of Artaxerxes the king [August 9, 449 B.C.E.]*

[Pledge:] *Ananiah son of Azariah, the lechen of Yahou the God who is in Elephantine the fortress, said to Meshullam son of Zakkur, Aramaean of Syene, of the military unit of Warizath: I have come to you that you might give to me in marriage Tamut, by name, who is your handmaiden. She is my wife and I am her husband from this day and forever.*

[Dowry:] *Tamut has brought to me in her hand,*
one garment of wool worth 7 shekels of silver,
one mirror worth 7½ hallur,
one pair of sandals
[ERASURE *one*] *half a handful of balsam ointment,*
6 handfuls of castor oil,
one tray.
All the money and the value of goods in money is 7 shekels and 7½ hallur.

[Divorce clause:] *If tomorrow or another day Anani[ah] rises up on account of her and says, "I divorce Tamut, my wife," the divorce money is on his head. He shall give to Tamut in silver 7 shekels, 2 quarters, and all that which she brought in her hand she shall take out, from straw to thread. If tomorrow or another day Tamut rises up and says, "I divorce my husband, Anani[ah]," a like sum will be on her head. She shall give to Anani[ah] 7 shekels, 2 quarters, and all that she brought in her hand she shall take out, from straw to thread.*

[Distribution of goods in event of death:] *If tomorrow or another day Ananiah should die, Tamut shall have power over all the goods which there may be between Anani[ah] and Tamut. If tomorrow or another day Tamut should die, Anani[ah] shall have power over all the goods which there may be between Tamut and Anani[ah].*

[Arrangements for their son:] *And I, Meshullam, tomorrow or another day, will not be able to take away Palti from under your heart except if*

Figure 13. *Marriage Document of Ananiah and Tamut.* From Elephantine Island, Egypt. July 3, 449 B.C.E. Ink on papyrus, 10⅜ × 12⅝ inches (26.5 × 32.2 cm). 47.218.89, Gift of Miss Theodora Wilbour

you drive out his mother, Tamut. And if I take
him away from you, I shall give to Anani[ah]
5 karsh of silver.

[Scribe and witnesses:] *Nathan son of Ananiah
wrote this document, and the witnesses to it
were Nathan son of Gaddul, Menahem son of
Zakkur, Gemariah son of Mahseiah.*

[Endorsement:] *Tamut brought in to Anani[ah]
in her hand silver, 1 karsh, 5 shekels.*

DEED OF EMANCIPATION

Freedom for Tamut and Yehoishema

Nearly twenty-two years after her marriage to Ananiah, Tamut's master released her and her daughter, Yehoishema, from slavery. It was rare for slaves to be freed. And though a slave could marry a free person, their children usually belonged to the master.

As an institution, slavery in Egypt at that time differed in notable ways from the practice in some other cultures: Egyptian slaves retained control over personal property, had professions, and were entitled to compensation. During the Persian Period in Egypt, it was not uncommon to sell children, or even oneself, into slavery to pay debts.

Translation:

[Date:] *On the 20th of Sivan [Aramaic calendar], that is the 7th day of Phamenoth [Egyptian calendar], the 38th year of Artaxerxes the king, [June 12, 427 B.C.E.]*

[Statement of Manumission:] *At that time, Meshullam son of Zakkur, a Jew of Elephantine the fortress and of the military unit of Iddinnabu, said to the lady Tamut, by name, upon whose hand is marked BELONGING TO MESHULLAM: I have thought of you in my lifetime. I have released you [effective] at my death, and I have released Yehoishema, by name, your daughter, whom you bore to me [as a matter of law]. My son or daughter, my brother or sister, near or far, partner-in-chattel or partner-in-land, shall not have power over you or over Yehoishema, your daughter, whom you bore to me [as a matter of law]. [No one] shall have power over you to mark you and to sell you for payment of silver. If anyone should rise up against you and against Yehoishema, your daughter, whom you bore to me [as a matter of law], he shall give to you a fine of silver, 50 karsh by the stone weight of the king.*

You are released from the shade to the sun, and also Yehoishema, your daughter. And another man shall have no power over you and Yehoishema, your daughter, but you are freed to God.

[Pledge to serve until Meshullam's death:] *Tamut and Yehoishema, her daughter, say: We will serve you as a son or daughter provides for his [or her] father in your lifetime and until your death. [And after your death] we will provide for Zakkur as the son provides for his father, just as we are serving you in your life.*

[Penalty for refusal:] *If we say, "We will not provide for you as a son provides for his father, or for Zakkur, your son, after your death," then we are liable to you and Zakkur, your son, for a fine of 50 karsh of silver, by royal weight, refined silver, without suit or process.*

[Scribe and witnesses:] *Haggai wrote this document in Elephantine at the dictation of Meshullam son of Zakkur, and the witnesses to it were: Atarparan son of Nisai the Mede, Micaiah son of Ahio, Berchiah son of Miptah, Delah son of Gaddul.*

[Endorsement:] *Document of withdrawal which Meshullam son of Zakkur wrote for Tamut and Yehoishema.*

Figure 14. *Freedom for Tamut and Yehoishema.* From Elephantine Island, Egypt. June 12, 427 B.C.E. Ink on papyrus, 15 × 12 inches (38.2 × 30.7 cm). 47.218.90, Gift of Miss Theodora Wilbour

REAL ESTATE DOCUMENTS

Bagazust and Ubil Sell a House to Ananiah

This document describes a property purchased by Ananiah, twelve years after his marriage, from a Persian soldier named Bagazust and his wife, Ubil. The property, in a town on Elephantine Island named for the god Khnum, was located across the street from the Temple of Yahou and next door to the Persian family of Ubil's father. As such proximity might suggest, the Egyptians, Jews, and Persians in Elephantine all lived among one another.

The renovation of the house and its gradual transfer to family members are the central concerns of the next several documents in Ananiah's family archive.

Translation:

[Date:] *On the 7th of Elul [Aramaic calendar], that is the 9th day of the month of Paoni [Egyptian calendar], the 28th year of Artaxerxes the king [September 14, 437 B.C.E.],*

[Participants:] *Bagazust son of Bazu, Caspian of the military unit of Namasava, and the woman Ubil the daughter of Satibar, Caspian of Syene of the military unit of Namasava, together one man and one woman said to Ananiah son of Azariah, lechen of Yahou the God,*

[Statement:] *We have sold and given to you the house of Apuly son of Misdai which is in Elephantine the fortress.*

[Description of house:] *The walls of it are standing. And a court is below. And it is not built upon. And it has windows. And it does not have beams.*

[Price:] *We have sold it to you and you gave to us its value in money, 1 karsh, 4 shekels in royal weight, 2 quarters in silver to the karsh, and our heart is satisfied at the price which you gave to us.*

[Description of boundaries:] *Look, these are the boundaries of that house which we sold to you. Above it is the house of Satibar. Below it is the way [or town] of Khnum [the Egyptian god] and the street of the king is between them. East of it is the treasury of the king adjoining it. On*
the west of it is the Temple of Yahou the God, and the street of the king is between them.

[Affirmation of sale:] *I, Bagazust, and Ubil, both of us, we have sold and given over to you and have removed [ourselves] from it from this day and forever. You, Ananiah son of Azariah, shall have power over that house and your children after you, and to anyone you wish to give it.*

[Promise not to sue:] *We shall not be able to start a suit or process against you regarding this house which we sold and gave to you and from which we removed [ourselves]. We shall not be able to sue your son or daughter, or anyone you wish to give it. If we start a suit or process against you or sue your son or daughter, or anyone you wish to give it, we shall give you in money 20 karsh silver, 2 quarters to the 10, and the house is also yours in addition and your children's after you, or anyone you wish to give it. Nor shall our son or daughter be able to start a suit or process in regard to this house whose boundaries are recorded above. If they start an action against you or bring actions against your son or daughter, they shall give to you in money 20 karsh silver, 2 quarters to the 10, and the house is also yours in addition and also your children's after you.*

[Assurance of clear title:] *And if another man sues you or sues your son or daughter, we will come forward and clear title and will give it to you within 30 days. And if we do not clear title, we or our children will give you a house like your house and its measurements, unless a son or daughter of Apuly come forward and we are not able to clear title. Then we will give to you your money, 1 karsh, 4 shekels, and the value of the building improvements which you have made in it, and all the fittings which may go into it.*

[Scribe and witnesses:] *Haggai son of Shemaiah wrote this at the dictation of Bagazust and Ubil. And the witnesses were Mithradata son of Mithrayazna; witness: Hyah son of Atarili, a Caspian, house of Ubil, a Caspian; witness: Aisaka son of Zamaspa.*

Figure 15. *Bagazust and Ubil Sell a House to Ananiah.* From Elephantine Island, Egypt. September 14, 437 B.C.E. Ink on papyrus, 31¾ × 11¾ inches (80.8 × 30.1 cm). 47.218.95, Gift of Miss Theodora Wilbour

Ananiah Gives Tamut Part of the House

Three years after purchasing the house from Bagazust and Ubil, Ananiah transferred ownership of an apartment within the now renovated house to his wife, Tamut. Although Tamut thereafter owned the apartment, Ananiah required that at her death it pass to their children, Palti and Yehoishema. As with all property transfers within a family, this gift was described as made "in love."

Translation:

[Date:] *On the 25th of Tishri [Aramaic calendar], that is the 25th of the month of Epiphi [Egyptian calendar] of the 31st year of Artaxerxes the king [October 30, 434 B.C.E.], Ananiah son of Azariah, lechen of the God Yahou in Elephantine the fortress, said to the woman Tamut, his wife,*

[Declaration:] *I give to you half of the room and its chamber of the house which I bought from Ubil the daughter of Satibar and from Bagazust, Caspians of Elephantine the fortress. I, Ananiah, have given it to you in love. It is yours from this day and forever and your children's, whom you bore to me.*

[Measurements:] *And these are the measurements of the house which I, Ananiah, have given to you, Tamut. From half of the room and its chamber it is 11 cubits from above to below by the one-cubit measure. It is 7 cubits and 1 hand from east to west in width by the one-cubit measure. In area it is 81 cubits.*

[Description:] *The lower part of the house is built new, having beams and windows.*

[Boundaries:] *And look, these are the boundaries of that house which I have given to you. Above it the portion which belongs to me—myself, Ananiah—adjoins it. Below it is the Temple of Yahou the God, and the street of the king is between them. East of it is the town of Khnum the god, and the street of the king is between them. On the west of it, the house of Satibar, the Caspian, adjoins it. This is the portion of the house, the measurements and boundaries of which are recorded above.*

[Promise not to sue:] *I, Ananiah, have given it to you in love. I am not able to start a suit against you on account of it. Neither shall my son, nor daughter, nor brother, nor sister be able to start a suit against you in regard to that house. And if I start a suit against you with regard to that house, I myself shall be liable and shall have to give you 5 karsh silver—that is five—by royal weight, 2 quarters silver to 1 karsh, and there shall be no suit. And if another man brings proceedings against you, he shall give to you 20 karsh silver, and the house in addition is yours.*

[Disposition of house at death:] *But if you die at the age of 100 years, my children whom you bore to me shall have power over it after your death. And moreover, if I, Anani[ah], shall die at the age of 100 years, Palti and Yehoishema, both of them my children, shall have power over my portion afterwards. I, Anani[ah], or another man, my mother or my father, my brother or sister, or another person, shall not have power over this house—any part of it—but my children whom you bore to me. And a man who would reclaim my house after my death from Palti and Yehoishema shall have to give them 10 karsh silver, by royal weight, 2 quarters to 1 karsh, and my house is theirs in addition. And there shall be no suit.*

[Scribe and witnesses:] *Mauziah son of Nathan wrote this at the dictation of Ananiah son of Azariah, the lechen. And the witnesses are: Gemariah son of Mahseiah, Hoshayah son of Yathom, Mithrasarah the Magian, Tatt the Magian.*

[Endorsement:] *Document of a house which Ananiah wrote for Tamut, his wife.*

Figure 16. *Ananiah Gives Tamut Part of the House.* From Elephantine Island, Egypt. October 30, 434 B.C.E. Ink on papyrus, 22½ × 11⅛ inches (57.1 × 28.4 cm). 47.218.91, Gift of Miss Theodora Wilbour

Ananiah Gives Yehoishema Part of the House

Drawn up thirty years after the preceding papyrus, this document is one of several that gradually transferred ownership of Ananiah and Tamut's house to their daughter, Yehoishema, as payment on her dowry.

The legal descriptions of the house preserve the names of Ananiah's neighbors. They included an Egyptian who held the post of gardener of the Egyptian god Khnum (mentioned below) and, on the other side, two Persian boatmen (see page 41).

Translation:

[Date:] *On the 24th of Marheshwan [Aramaic date], that is the 29th day of Mesore [Egyptian date], the 1st year of Artaxerxes [II] the king [November 25, 404 B.C.E.]*

[Declaration:] *At that time Anani[ah] son of Azariah, lechen of Yahou the God in Elephantine the fortress, said to the woman Yehoishema, his daughter, I have taken thought of you in my life and I have given to you part of my house which I bought with silver and whose price I gave. I have given to you the southern room, east of my large room, and half the court, that is half the hayet [as it is called] in Egyptian, and half the empty space beneath the stairway which is the storage area.*

[Measurements:] *These are the measurements of the house which I gave to Yehoishema, my daughter, in love. These are the measurements of the house which I, Anani[ah] gave to Yehoishema, my daughter. From the lower side to the upper it is 8 cubits and a half by the one-cubit measure, and from east to west 7 cubits by the one-cubit measure, in area 98 cubits by the one-cubit measure, and in addition half the court and half the stairs, and the storage area.*

[Boundaries:] *And these are the boundaries of the house which I gave to Yehoishema, my daughter. East of it is the protecting wall which the Egyptians built, that is "the way of the god" [in Egyptian]. Above it, the house of "the shrine of the god" [in Egyptian] adjoins it wall to wall. Below it is the wall of the stairway, and the*

house of Hor son of Petesi, gardener of the god Khnum, adjoins that staircase. West of it is the wall of the large room.

[Transfer:] *It is yours. You shall have power over it. This is the house whose measurements and boundaries are written in this document. I, Anani[ah] son of Azariah, gave it to you in love.*

[Description:] *The construction of the lower house has beams and there are 3 windows in it, one door in it, shutting and opening.*

[Further rights:] *Moreover, you shall have power over the lower part—that is the court— you shall have power to prop up what is knocked over and what is falling in your half. Moreover, you shall have power to go out the gate of the lower part, that is the court. Moreover, you shall have power over half the stairs to go up and come down. This is the house whose boundaries and measurements are written and its words are written in this document.*

[Transfer:] *I, Anani[ah], give it to Yehoishema, my daughter, at my death in love, because she did take care of me when I was old in days and not able to work with my hands, and she did maintain me. Moreover, I give it to her at my death.*

[Promise not to sue:] *My son, nor my daughter, my partner-in-chattel, my partner-in-land, my guarantor will not be able to bring suit or action against you. Nor shall anyone start it against your children after you and bring complaint against you before the prefect or lord or against your children after you.*

[Penalty for suit:] *Anyone who brings a suit or action against you or against your children shall give to you a fine of 30 karsh of silver, royal weight, refined silver.*

[Clear title:] *And you, Yehoishema, shall have power and your children shall have power after you, and to whomever you shall give it. Moreover, they shall not be able to bring forth against you a document, new or old, except this document which I made out to you that is valid.*

[Scribe and witnesses:] *Haggai son of Shemaiah wrote this document in Elephantine the fortress at the dictation of Anani[ah] son of Azariah, the lechen of Yahou the God. Witnesses to it: Hashiah son of Yathom, Zakkur son of Shallum, Nathan son of Yehoor, Hoshiah son of Nathan, Meshullam son of Mauzi, Palti son of Yeush, Yoshibiah son of Yedoniah, Haggai son of Mardu.*

[Endorsement:] *Document concerning a house, which Anani[ah] son of Azariah, the lechen, wrote to Yehoishema, his daughter.*

Figure 17. *Ananiah Gives Yehoishema Part of the House.* From Elephantine Island, Egypt. November 26, 404 B.C.E. Ink on papyrus, 27¼ × 12⅛ inches (69.3 × 30.9 cm). 47.218.92, Gift of Miss Theodora Wilbour

Ananiah Gives Yehoishema Another Part of the House

For his daughter Yehoishema's dowry, Ananiah had transferred to her partial ownership of the house he shared with Tamut. After making more repairs to the building, Ananiah transferred a further section of the house, described in this document, to the dowry.

Translation:

[Date:] *On the 20th of Adar [Aramaic calendar], that is the 8th day of Koihak [Egyptian calendar], the 3rd year of Artaxerxes the king [March 9, 402 B.C.E.]*

[Transfer:] *At that time, Anani[ah] son of Azariah, the lechen of Yahou the God in Elephantine the fortress, said to Yehoishema, his daughter: I have given to you a house.*

[Description:] *The construction of the lower part of the house has beams and there are three doors. Its stairway and courtyard are built, that is, its exit gate.*

[Boundaries:] *And these are its boundaries. East of it, the treasury of the king adjoins wall to wall the "protecting wall" [in Egyptian] which the Egyptians built. West of it is your gate to go out, and the street of the king is between them. Above it, the house of the "shrine of the god" [in Egyptian] adjoins it wall to wall, and the wall of its house adjoins it, that is, my large room. Below it, the house of Hor son of Petesi, the gardener of Khnum the god, adjoins it wall to wall.*

[Immediate transfer of title:] *This is the house of which the boundaries are written in this document. I, Anani[ah] son of Azariah, gave it to you as an addition which is not written in the document of your marriage with Anani[ah] son of Haggai, son of Meshullam, son of Beses. You, Yehoishema, my daughter, shall have power over it from this day and forever. I, Anani[ah] son of Azariah, shall not be able to say, "I gave it to you in love as an addition not written in the document of your marriage at another time." If I say, "I will take it away from you," I will be liable and will have to give Yehoishema a fine of silver, 30 karsh, refined silver in royal weight.*

And you shall have power over this house, the boundaries of which are written above, in my life and at my death.

[Promise not to sue:] *Moreover, if my son or my daughter, brother, sister, partner-in-chattel, partner-in-land, or guarantor starts a suit or process against you and brings a complaint against you and your children to a prefect or lord to remove this house from you in my lifetime or at my death, then such a person shall be liable and shall give to you and your children a fine of silver, 30 karsh by royal weight. In addition you shall have power over this house whose boundaries are written in this document. If he goes into court, he shall not win.*

[No other documents should be considered valid:] *Moreover, they shall not be able to put forth against you a document new or old in the name of this house of which the boundaries were written above in this document. That document would be false. This document, which I, Anani[ah] wrote for you, is valid.*

[Scribe and witnesses:] *Haggai son of Shemaiah wrote this document in Elephantine at the dictation of Anani[ah] son of Azariah, the lechen of Yahou the God. Witnesses to it: Nathan son of Yehoor, Menahem son of Gaddul, Rehum son of Beitha, Nathan son of Mauziyah, Shammu son of Pilpeliah, Haggai son of Mardu, Yedoniah son of Gemariah.*

[Endorsement:] *Document of the house which Anani[ah] son of Azariah wrote to Yehoishema, his daughter.*

Figure 18. *Ananiah Gives Yehoishema Another Part of the House.* From Elephantine Island, Egypt. March 10, 402 B.C.E. Ink on papyrus, 17 × 12¾ inches (43.4 × 32.7 cm). 47.218.88, Gift of Miss Theodora Wilbour

Figure 19. Antonio Beato (British, 1825–1903). *View of Elephantine Island with Roman Structures* (detail), circa 1870. Albumen print, 10¾ x 14¹¹⁄₁₆ inches (26 x 37.3 cm). 293, Department of Prints, Drawings, and Photographs

Ananiah and Tamut Sell the House to Their Son-in-Law

This papyrus records the sale of the remaining portion of Ananiah and Tamut's house to Yehoishema's husband. Possibly because the clients were dissatisfied with something the scribe had written, at one point the text of the document breaks off and then starts over again, repeating what has gone before with some additions. The boundary description included here refers to the Temple of Yahou in Elephantine, now rebuilt eight years after its destruction in 410 B.C.E. during a civil conflict that arose out of a land dispute.

Translation:

[Date:] *On the 12th of Thoth [Egyptian date], the 4th year of Artaxerxes the king [December 13, 402 B.C.E.]*

[Declaration:] *At that time Anani[ah] son of Azariah, the lechen of Yahou, and the lady Tamut, his wife, lechenah of Yahou the God who dwells in Elephantine the fortress, said to Anani[ah] son of Haggai, son of Meshullam, son of Beses, Aramaean of Elephantine the fortress of the military unit of Nabukudurri: I and Tamut the daughter of Pethu, the two of us, have sold and given over to you our house which we bought with silver from Bagazust son of Palyn, Caspian, that is the house of Yanbuli son of Misdai, Caspian, which he possessed in Elephantine. And you gave to us the price of our house in money: one, that is 1 karsh, three, that is 3 shekels, in Ionian Greek silver, that is 6 staters, one shekel. Our hearts are satisfied with it, that there is not outstanding to us against you any part of the price.*

[Measurements:] *These are the measurements of the house which we sold and gave over to you. From the east to west, a length of 16 cubits and 2 hands by the one-cubit measure. And from below to above a width of 5 cubits and 2 hands by the one-cubit measure. In area 150 cubits.*

[Boundaries:] *And these are the boundaries of the house which we sold and gave over to you. On the east of it is the house which I gave to you as an addition.*

[Here the document repeats from the beginning with some additions.]

[Date:] *On the 12th of Thoth [Egyptian date], the 4th year of Artaxerxes the king [December 13, 402 B.C.E.]*

[Declaration:] *At that time Anani[ah] son of Azariah, lechen of Yahou the God, and Tamut, his wife, [formerly] chief beloved [in Persian] of Meshullam son of Zakkur, both of them in full agreement, said to Anani[ah] son of Haggai, son of Beses: We sold and gave over to you our house which we bought from Bagazust son of Palyn, a Caspian.*

[Description:] *The lower house is a construction having beams, windows, and 2 doors. The construction of the lower house consists of my large room.*

[Price:] *And you gave us the price in silver one karsh, 3 shekels—Ionian Greek silver 6 staters, 1 shekel. And our heart is satisfied at the price which you have given to us.*

[Measurements:] *These are the measurements of the house which we sold and gave over to you. From east to west the length of cubits is 16 cubits and 2 hands by the one-cubit measure and from above to below the width is 5 cubits and 2 hands by the one-cubit measure. And the area is 151 cubits and 1 hand.*

[Boundaries:] *These are the boundaries of the house which we sold and gave over to you. East of it is your house, Anani[ah] son of Haggai, which we gave to Yehoishema as an additional*

portion on the document of her marriage, which adjoins it wall to wall. On the west of it is the Temple of Yahou, and the street of the king is between them. Above it, the house of Parnu son of Zili and Mardu, his brother, adjoins it wall to wall. Below it is the house of Pehi and Pemet, his brother, boatmen of the waters, the sons of Tawi, and the street of the king is between them, and its one window opens to the large room, and the gate above opens to the street of the king. From there you will exit and enter the house of which the measurements and boundaries are recorded in this document.

[Clear title:] *You, Anani[ah son of Haggai], shall have power over it from this day and forever. And your children shall have power after you. And anyone to whom you give it and to whom you will sell it for money.*

[Promise not to sue:] *I, Anani[ah], and Tamut, my wife, who was handmaiden to Meshullam son of Zakkur, who gave her to me in marriage, we shall not be able to start a suit or a process against you with mention of this house which we sold and gave over to you and for which you gave us its price in silver and our heart was satisfied with it. Moreover, we shall not be able to start a suit against your sons and your daughters or whomever you may give it for money or as a gift. Moreover, our sons and daughters, our partners-in-chattel, partners-in-land, and guar-* antors, *shall not be able to sue. Whoever shall start a suit against you or your children or anyone to whom you have given it, and whoever brings a complaint against you to a prefect or lord or judge with mention of this house of which the measurements are written above, or anyone who raises a document, new or old, with mention of this house which we have sold, against you, [they] shall be liable and shall give to you or your children a fine of silver, 20 karsh, royal weight, refined silver. And the house is yours and your children's and whomever you have given it as a gift.*

[Transfer of old document:] *Moreover, we have given to you the old document which Bagazust wrote to us as document of sale which he sold to us and we gave him its price in silver.*

[Scribe and witnesses:] *Haggai son of Shemaiah wrote this document at the dictation of Anani[ah], lechen of Yahou the God, and Tamut the daughter of Pethu, his wife, both of them in full accord. Witnesses: Meshullam son of Mauziah, Rehum son of Beitha, Nathan son of Yehoor.*

[Endorsement:] *Document concerning the house which Anani[ah] son of Azariah and Tamut, his wife, did sell.*

Figure 20. *Ananiah and Tamut Sell the House to Their Son-in-Law.* From Elephantine Island, Egypt. December 13, 402 B.C.E. Ink on papyrus, 24 × 12½ inches (61.4 × 31.8 cm). 47.218.94, Gift of Miss Theodora Wilbour

LOAN AGREEMENT

Receipt for a Grain Loan

Sometime in December 402 B.C.E., Ananiah son of Haggai borrowed two monthly rations of grain from Pakhnum son of Besa, an Aramaean with an Egyptian name. This receipt would have been held by Pakhnum and returned to Ananiah son of Haggai when he repaid the loan. No interest is charged, but there is a penalty for failing to repay the loan by the agreed date.

The receipt demonstrates that friendly business relations continued between Egyptians and Jews in Elephantine after the expulsion of the Persians by the kings of Dynasty 28.

Translation:

[Date:] *Month of Thoth [Egyptian calendar], year 4 of Artaxerxes [Persian calendar], the king at that time in Syene [December 402 B.C.E.].*

[Parties and loan amount:] *Anani[ah] son of Haggai, son of Meshullam, a Jew of the military unit of Nabukudurri, said to Pakhnum son of Besa, an Aramaean of Syene of the military unit: I came to you in your house in Syene the fortress. I borrowed from you and you gave to me 2 peras [an unknown measurement] and 3 seahs [30 quarts] of emmer wheat. Later, I, Anani[ah] son of Haggai, will pay back and give to you that emmer wheat, 2 peras and 3 seahs, from the ration which will be given to me from the treasury of the king.*

[In case of default:] *And if I do not pay back and give to you that emmer wheat which is written above, when the ration is given to me from the treasury of the king, then I, Anani[ah], shall be liable to pay you a fine of one (1) karsh, refined silver. Thereafter, I, Anani[ah], will pay and give to you the fine which is written above within 20 days—that is twenty—and without suit.*

[In case of death of borrower:] *And if I die and have not yet paid back and given to you your silver which is written above, then my children and my guarantors will pay you your silver which is written above.*

[Security:] *And if my children and my guarantors do not pay you this silver which is written above, then you, Pakhnum, shall have power over my children tomorrow and shall take for yourself from the house belonging to the children [from among the following]: slave, handmaiden, vessels of copper and iron, clothing and produce, what you will find belonging to me in Elephantine and in Syene or in the province until you receive the money which is written above, without suit.*

[Scribe:] *Shewahram son of Eshemram, son of Eshemzebed, wrote this document in Syene the fortress at the dictation of Anani[ah] son of Haggai, son of Meshullam.*

[Witnesses:] *Menahem son of Shallum; Haggai; Rehum son of Beitha; Haggai son of Mardu.*

[Endorsement:] *Document of grain which [Anani[ah] son of Haggai] son of Meshullam [wrote] for Pakhnum son of Besa.*

Figure 21. *Receipt for a Grain Loan.* From Elephantine Island, Egypt. December 402 B.C.E. Ink on papyrus, 13¾ × 12 inches (34.8 × 30.5 cm). 47.218.93, Gift of Miss Theodora Wilbour

CHRONOLOGY

Jewish Life in Ancient Egypt: The Historical Context

Circa 1650 B.C.E. Joseph enters Egypt.

Circa 1250 B.C.E. Moses leads the Exodus from Egypt.

Circa 1210 B.C.E. Joshua leads the settlement of Canaan.

1030–931 B.C.E. The United Monarchy of Judah, Israel, and Jerusalem is ruled, successively, by the kings Saul, David, and Solomon.

931 B.C.E. The Monarchy is divided into the Kingdom of Israel and the Kingdom of Judah.

722 B.C.E. The Kingdom of Israel falls to the Assyrians; some Jews may go to Egypt.

586 B.C.E. Jerusalem and Judah fall to the Babylonians; the First Temple is destroyed; Jews go into exile in Babylonia and Egypt.

539 BCE – Persians conquer Babylonians

536 B.C.E. The Persian King Cyrus permits construction of the Second Temple in Jerusalem.

525 B.C.E. The Persians conquer Egypt.

449–402 B.C.E. **Period encompassed by the archive of Ananiah and Tamut, the focus of *Jewish Life in Ancient Egypt*.**

404 B.C.E. The Persians are expelled from Egypt.

343–332 B.C.E. Brief return of Persian rule in Egypt.

332 B.C.E. Alexander the Great conquers Egypt.

Further Reading

Kraeling, Emil G. *The Brooklyn Museum Aramaic Papyri: New Documents of the Fifth Century B.C. from the Jewish Colony at Elephantine.* New Haven: Published for The Brooklyn Museum by Yale University Press, 1953.

Porten, Bezalel. *Archives from Elephantine: The Life of an Ancient Jewish Military Colony.* Berkeley and Los Angeles: University of California Press, 1968.

Porten, Bezalel, et al. *The Elephantine Papyri in English: Three Millennia of Cross-Cultural Continuity and Change.* Leiden: E. J. Brill, 1996.